Sizzle!

A Book About Heat Waves

NEXT EXIT
3 MILES

By Rick Thomas
Illustrated by Denise Shea

Content Adviser: Daniel Dix, Senior Meteorologist,
The Weather Channel

Reading Adviser: Susan Kesselring, M.A., Literacy Educator,
Rosemount-Apple Valley-Eagan (Minnesota) School District

PICTURE WINDOW BOOKS
Minneapolis, Minnesota

Managing Editor: Catherine Neitge
Creative Director: Terri Foley
Art Director: Keith Griffin
Editor: Patricia Stockland
Designer: Nathan Gassman
Page production: Picture Window Books
The illustrations in this book were
prepared digitally.

Picture Window Books
5115 Excelsior Boulevard
Suite 232
Minneapolis, MN 55416
877-845-8392
www.picturewindowbooks.com

Printed in the United States of America.

Library of Congress Cataloging-in-Publication Data
Thomas, Rick, 1954-
Sizzle! : a book about heat waves / by Rick Thomas ;
illustrated by Denise Shea.
p. cm. — (Amazing science)
Includes bibliographical references and index.
ISBN 1-4048-0927-9 (hardcover)
1. Heat waves (Meteorology)—Juvenile
literature. 2. Heat–Physiological effect—
Juvenile literature. I. Shea, Denise. II. Title.
III. Series.

QC981.8.A5T46 2004
551.5'253—dc22
2004019189

Table of Contents

A blazing sun burns in a hot sky. There are no clouds, no rain, no cooling breezes.

The city bakes in a heat wave.

Heat Wave

When both air temperature and humidity are high and last for more than three days, weather experts call it a heat wave.

During a heat wave, thermometers show high air temperatures. Air always holds water vapor. But when the humidity is high, there is more water vapor in the air. Humidity measures the wetness of the air. The hot, damp air makes your skin feel sticky and uncomfortable.

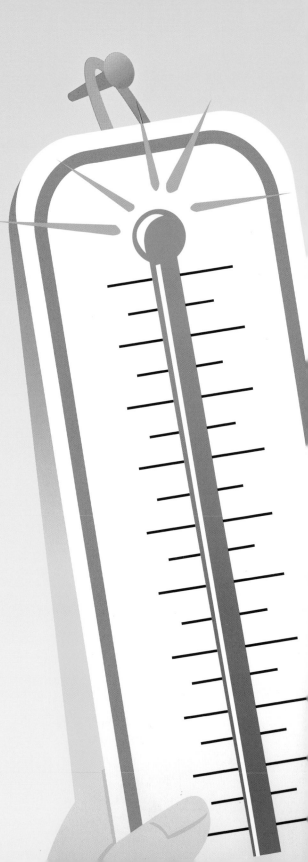

Heat Index

The sun beats down on sidewalks and streets. Door handles on cars feel as hot as burners on a stove. Touching metal furniture or mailboxes can blister your skin. It even feels warm in the shade.

How warm will you feel in the hot weather? Check the heat index. It is the combination of high temperature and humidity. When the heat index is above 115 degrees Fahrenheit, the air is dangerously hot. Standing in direct sunlight can cause a person's heat index to rise 15 more degrees!

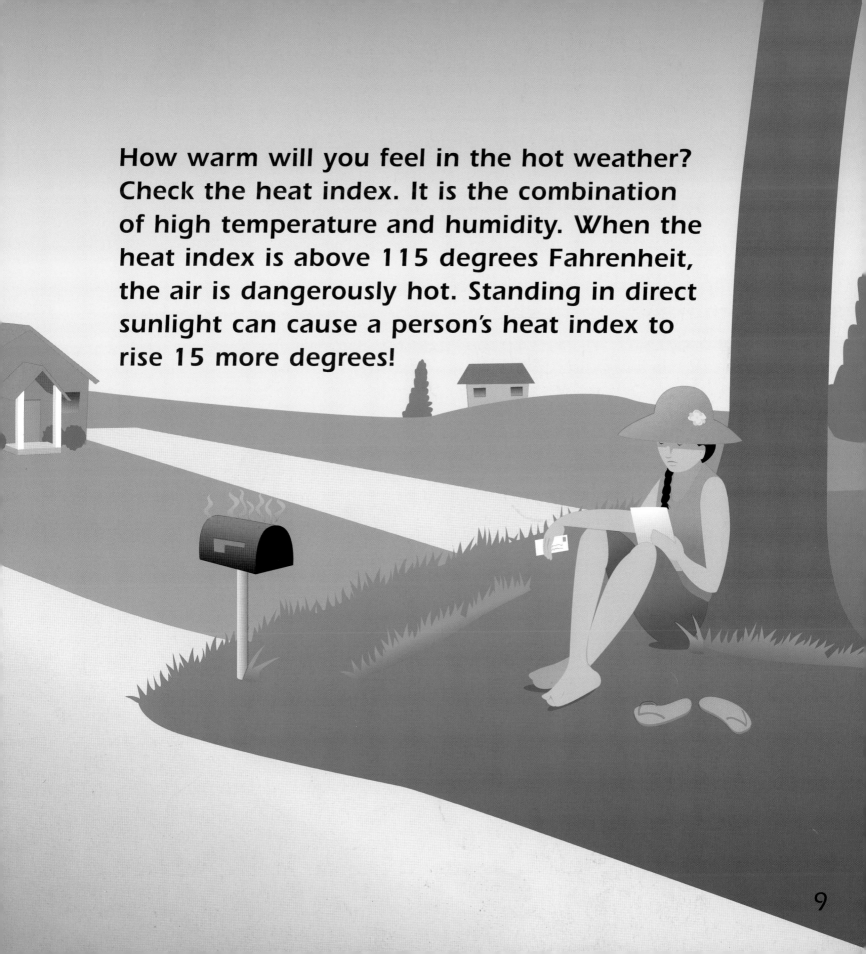

City Heat

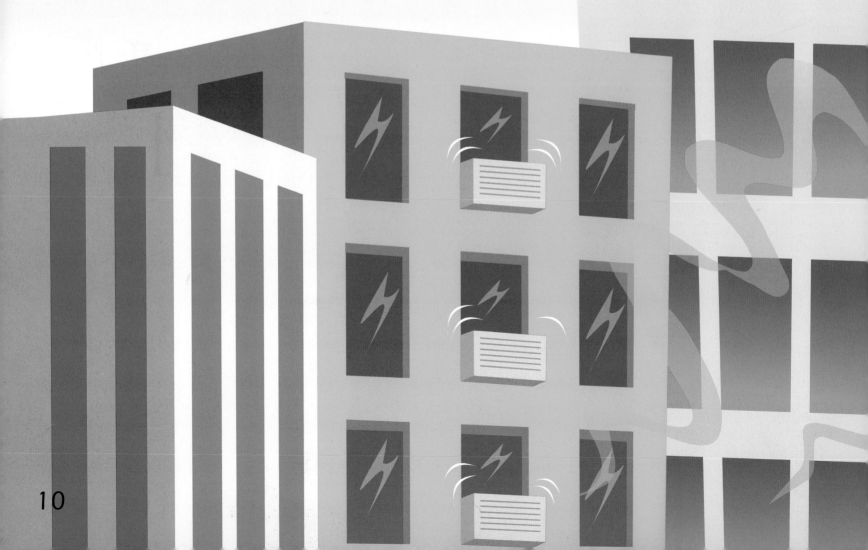

Heat waves threaten big cities.

Tall buildings jammed next to one another block out cooling winds. Busy air conditioners pump more heat into alleys and streets. City workers sweat in the hot, humid air.

11

Water Shortage

In a long heat wave, the ground can also lose water. Grass grows brown, and flowers fade. People use water sprinklers and hoses to refresh their yards and gardens. But these use up more and more water.

Without rain, there is no water to fill up lakes, rivers, city water towers, and wells. No fountains run, no swimming pools splash, no ice cubes clink, no faucets drip.

Country Heat

In the countryside, the hot sun causes the water in lakes and ponds to evaporate. The water rises into the air as steam.

With less water, the lakes and ponds sink lower and lower. Underground wells, which supply water for drinking, dry up.

Fire Hazards

Without enough water, trees, plants, and grass grow brittle and dry. A small spark could easily set them on fire. But a low water supply means not enough water to fight fires.

Special bans or rules are set up to prevent fires during extremely hot weather. Tourists in parks and forests are banned from building campfires.

17

Drought

When the heat wave lasts for many months or a full season, the weather can cause a deadly drought. The glaring sun dries up streams and creeks. The thirsty ground dries up and cracks. Farm crops wither and wilt in the fields.

NEXT EXIT
3 MILES

Without enough water, plants stop growing.
Without enough water, animals die.

19

Stay cool in the warm shade. Take off your shoes and socks. Drink lots of water. Rub an ice cube against your neck.

Maybe tomorrow it will rain and cool off. Maybe tomorrow the heat wave will break.

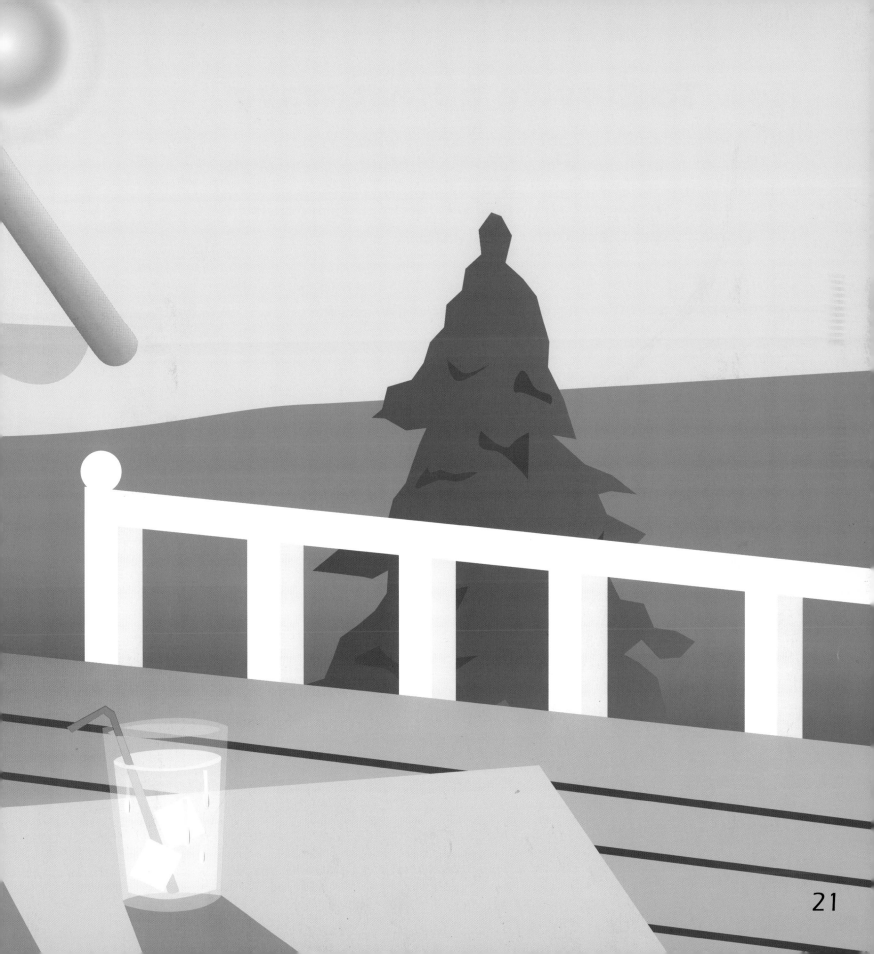

How To Survive a Heat Wave

It is important to keep cool during a heat wave. Watch for signs of heat sickness in yourself and others. These signs include dizziness, vomiting, lots of sweating, rapid breathing, and rapid heartbeat. If you notice any of these signs, call 911. Don't forget these other safety tips.

- Drink lots of water. Most health experts say people should drink about seven or eight glasses of water a day.

- Don't drink beverages with caffeine, such as soda pop or tea. It causes your body to lose water.

- Stay indoors and out of the sun.

- Wear light, cool clothes.

- Eat smaller meals, and eat more often. Big meals will heat up your body.

- Slow down. Don't play or work the same way you would in cooler weather. Your body needs time to cool off.

- Don't forget your pets! Make sure they have enough water to drink. If you can, keep them indoors, out of the sun.

Extreme Storm Extras

- Your body sweats to cool itself. Beads of perspiration, or sweat, run out of the tiny pores on your skin. The salty water makes your skin damp. Air feels cooler against the wet skin.

- Train engineers must drive carefully over hot tracks. Train wheels can spark and send small flames into dry, grassy fields.

- High heat can cause train tracks to bend and buckle. During heat waves, trains might stop running due to damaged tracks.

- In the summer of 2003, hot weather sizzled over France. Thousands of farm animals died throughout the countryside and hundreds of people died in the capital city of Paris.

- Heat exhaustion, heat cramps, and heatstroke, also called sunstroke, are heat sicknesses that can strike humans.

Glossary

banned—not allowed

droplets—tiny drops of a liquid

evaporate—how water leaves things, usually as a vapor or steam

hazard—something that is dangerous; a risk of danger

humidity—a measure of how much water is in the air

perspiration—sweat

To Learn More

At the Library

Burby, Liza. *Heatwaves and Droughts.*
New York: PowerKids Press, 1999.

Chambers, Catherine. *Heatwave.* Chicago,
Ill.: Heinemann Library, 2002.

Hewitt, Sally. *Weather.* New York: Children's
Press, 2000.

On the Web

FactHound offers a safe, fun way to find
Web sites related to this book. All of the
sites on FactHound have been researched
by our staff. *www.facthound.com*

1. Visit the FactHound home page.
2. Enter a search word related to this book,
   or type in this special code: 1404809279
3. Click on the FETCH IT button.

Your trusty FactHound will fetch the best
sites for you!

Index

Look for all of the books in this series:

Eye of the Storm: A Book About Hurricanes
Flakes and Flurries: A Book About Snow
Gusts and Gales: A Book About Wind
Nature's Fireworks: A Book About Lightning
Rising Waters: A Book About Floods
Rumble, Boom! A Book About Thunderstorms
Shapes in the Sky: A Book About Clouds
Sizzle! A Book About Heat Waves
Splish! Splash! A Book About Rain
Sunshine: A Book About Sunlight
Twisters: A Book About Tornadoes
Whiteout! A Book About Blizzards